TOUGH
QUESTIONS
REVISED EDITION

# HOW DOES ANYONE KNOW GOD EXISTS?

# The Tough Questions Series

*How Does Anyone Know God Exists?* by Garry Poole

*What Difference Does Jesus Make?* by Judson Poling

*How Reliable Is the Bible?* by Judson Poling

*How Could God Allow Suffering and Evil?* by Garry Poole

*Don't All Religions Lead to God?* by Garry Poole

*Do Science and the Bible Conflict?* by Judson Poling

*Why Become a Christian?* by Garry Poole

*Tough Questions Leader's Guide* by Garry Poole and Judson Poling

**TOUGH QUESTIONS**

REVISED EDITION

HOW DOES

ANYONE

KNOW GOD

EXISTS?

# HOW DOES ANYONE KNOW GOD EXISTS?

## GARRY POOLE

*foreword by* **Lee Strobel**

**ZONDERVAN**®

WILLOW
Willow Creek Resources

ZONDERVAN.com/
AUTHORTRACKER
*follow your favorite authors*

We want to hear from you. Please send your comments about this book
to us in care of zreview@zondervan.com. Thank you.

**ZONDERVAN®**

*How Does Anyone Know God Exists?*
Copyright © 1998, 2003 by Willow Creek Association

Requests for information should be addressed to:

Zondervan, *Grand Rapids, Michigan 49530*

ISBN: 0-310-24502-8

*Interior design by Nancy Wilson*

*Printed in the United States of America*

03 04 05 06 07 08 09 / CH / 10 9 8 7 6 5 4 3 2 1

# Contents

# Foreword

For most of my life I was an atheist. I thought that the Bible was hopelessly riddled with mythology, that God was a man-made creation born of wishful thinking, and that the deity of Jesus was merely a product of legendary development. My no-nonsense education in journalism and law contributed to my skeptical viewpoint. In fact, just the idea of an all-powerful, all-loving, all-knowing creator of the universe seemed too absurd to even justify the time to investigate whether there could be any evidence backing it up.

However, my agnostic wife's conversion to Christianity, and the subsequent transformation of her character and values, prompted me to launch my own spiritual journey in 1980. Using the skills I developed as the legal affairs editor of *The Chicago Tribune,* I began to check out whether any concrete facts, historical data, or convincing logic supported the Christian faith. Looking back, I wish I had this curriculum to supplement my efforts.

This excellent material can help you in two ways. If you're already a Christ-follower, this series can provide answers to some of the tough questions your seeker friends are asking—or you're asking yourself. If you're not yet following Christ but consider yourself either an open-minded skeptic or a spiritual seeker, this series can also help you in your journey. You can thoroughly and responsibly explore the relevant issues while discussing the topics in community with others. In short, it's a tremendous guide for people who really want to discover the truth about God and this fascinating and challenging Nazarene carpenter named Jesus.

If the previous paragraph describes you in some way, then prepare for the adventure of a lifetime. Let the pages that follow take you on a stimulating journey of discovery as you grapple with the most profound—and potentially life-changing—questions in the world.

—Lee Strobel, author of
*The Case for Christ* and *The Case for Faith*

# Getting Started

Welcome to the Tough Questions series! This small group curriculum was produced with the conviction that claims regarding spiritual truth can and should be tested. Religions—sometimes considered exempt from scrutiny—are not free to make sweeping declarations and demands without providing solid reasons why they should be taken seriously. These teachings, including those from the Bible in particular, purport to explain the most significant of life's mysteries, with consequences alleged to be eternal. Such grand claims should be analyzed carefully. If this questioning process exposes faulty assertions, it only makes sense to refuse to place one's trust in these flawed systems of belief. If, on the other hand, an intense investigation leads to the discovery of truth, the search will have been worth it all.

Christianity contends that God welcomes sincere examination and inquiry; in fact, it's a matter of historical record that Jesus encouraged such scrutiny. The Bible is not a secret kept only for the initiated few, but an open book available for study and debate. The central teachings of Christianity are freely offered to all, to the skeptic as well as to the believer.

So here's an open invitation: explore the options, examine the claims, and draw your conclusions. And once you encounter and embrace the truth—look out! Meaningful life-change and growth will be yours to enjoy.

It is possible for any of us to believe error; it is also feasible for us to resist truth. Using this set of discussion guides will help you sort out the true from the supposed, and ultimately offer a reasonable defense of the Christian faith. Whether you are a nonbeliever or

> You will seek me and find me when you seek me with all your heart.
>
> —Jeremiah 29:13

9

skeptic, or someone who is already convinced and looking to fortify your faith, these guides will lead you to a fascinating exploration of vital spiritual truths.

## Tough Questions for Small Groups

The Tough Questions series is specifically designed to give spiritual seekers (or non-Christians) a chance to raise questions and investigate the basics of the Christian faith within the safe context of a seeker small group. These groups typically consist of a community of two to twelve seekers and one or two leaders who gather on a regular basis, primarily to discuss spiritual matters. Seeker groups meet at a wide variety of locations, from homes and offices to restaurants and churches to bookstores and park district picnic tables. A trained Christian leader normally organizes the group and facilitates the discussions based on the seekers' spiritual concerns and interests. Usually, at least one apprentice (or coleader) who is also a Christian assists the group leader. The rest of the participants are mostly, if not all, non-Christians. This curriculum is intended to enhance these seeker small group discussions and create a fresh approach to exploring the Christian faith.

Because the primary audience is the not-yet-convinced seeker, these guides are designed to represent the skeptical, along with the Christian, perspective. While the truths of the Christian position are strongly affirmed, it is anticipated that non-Christians will dive into these materials with a group of friends and discover that their questions and doubts are not only well understood and represented here, but also valued. If that goal is accomplished, open and honest discussions about Christianity can follow. The greatest hope behind the formation of this series is that seekers will be challenged in a respectful way to seriously consider and even accept the claims of Christ.

A secondary purpose behind the design of this series is to provide a tool for small groups of Christians to use as they discuss answers to the tough questions seekers are asking. The process of wrestling through these important questions and issues will not only strengthen their own personal faith but also provide them with insights for entering into informed dialogues about Christianity with their seeking friends.

A hybrid of the two options mentioned above may make more sense for some groups. For example, a small group of Christians may want to open up their discussion to include those who are just beginning to investigate spiritual things. This third approach provides an excellent opportunity for both Christians and seekers to examine the claims of Christianity together. Whatever the configuration of your group, may you benefit greatly as you use these guides to fully engage in lively discussions about issues that matter most.

## Guide Features

### The Introduction

At the beginning of every session is an introduction, usually several paragraphs long. You may want to read this beforehand even though your leader will probably ask the group to read it aloud together at the start of every meeting. These introductions are written from a skeptical point of view, so a full spectrum of perspectives is represented in each session. Hopefully, this information will help you feel represented, understood, and valued.

### Open for Discussion

Most sessions contain ten to fifteen questions your group can discuss. You may find that it is difficult for your group to get through all these questions in one sitting. That is okay; the important thing is to engage in the topic at hand—not to necessarily get through every question. Your group, however, may decide to spend more than one meeting on each session in order to address all of the questions. The Open for Discussion sections are designed to draw out group participation and give everyone the opportunity to process things openly.

Usually, the first question of each session is an "icebreaker." These simple questions are designed to get the conversation going by prompting the group to discuss a nonthreatening issue, usually having to do with the session topic to be covered. Your group may want to make time for additional icebreakers at the beginning of each discussion.

### Heart of the Matter

The section called "Heart of the Matter" represents a slight turn in the group discussion. Generally speaking, the questions in this section speak more to the emotional, rather than just the intellectual, side of the issue. This is an opportunity to get in touch with how you feel about a certain aspect of the topic being discussed and to share those feelings with the rest of the group.

### Charting Your Journey

The purpose of the "Charting Your Journey" section is to challenge you to go beyond a mere intellectual and emotional discussion to personal application. This group experience is, after all, a journey, so each session includes this section devoted to helping you identify and talk about your current position. Your views will most likely fluctuate as you make new discoveries along the way.

### Straight Talk

Every session has at least one section, called "Straight Talk," designed to stimulate further thinking and discussion around relevant supplementary information. The question immediately following Straight Talk usually refers to the material just presented, so it is important that you read and understand this part before you attempt to answer the question.

### Quotes

Scattered throughout every session are various quotes, many of them from skeptical or critical points of view. These are simply intended to spark your thinking about the issue at hand.

### Scripture for Further Study

This section ends each session with a list of suggested Scripture passages that relate to the discussion topic.

### Recommended Resources

This section at the back of each guide lists recommended books that may serve as helpful resources for further study.

## Discussion Guidelines

These guides, which consist mainly of questions to be answered in your group setting, are designed to elicit dialogue rather than short, simple answers. Strictly speaking, these guides are not Bible studies, though they regularly refer to biblical themes and passages. Instead, they are topical discussion guides, meant to get you talking about what you really think and feel. The sessions have a point and attempt to lead to some resolution, but they fall short of providing the last word on any of the questions raised. That is left for you to discover for yourself! You will be invited to bring your experience, perspective, and uncertainties to the discussion, and you will also be encouraged to compare your beliefs with what the Bible teaches in order to determine where you stand as each meeting unfolds.

Your group should have a discussion leader. This facilitator can get needed background material for each session in the *Tough Questions Leader's Guide*. There, your leader will find some brief points of clarification and understanding (along with suggested answers) for many of the questions in each session. The supplemental book *Seeker Small Groups* is also strongly recommended as a helpful resource for leaders to effectively start up small groups and facilitate discussions for spiritual seekers. *The Complete Book of Questions: 1001 Conversation Starters for Any Occasion,* a resource filled with icebreaker questions, may be a useful tool to assist everyone in your group to get to know one another better, and to more easily launch your interactions.

In addition, keep the following list of suggestions in mind as you prepare to participate in your group discussions.

1. The Tough Questions series does not necessarily need to be discussed sequentially. The guides, as well as individual sessions, can be mixed and matched in any order and easily discussed independently of each other, based on everyone's interests and questions.

2. If possible, read over the material before each meeting. Familiarity with the topic will greatly enrich the time you spend in the group discussion.

3. Be willing to join in the group interaction. The leader of the group will not present a lecture but rather will encourage each of you to openly discuss your opinions and disagreements. Plan to share your ideas honestly and forthrightly.

4. Be sensitive to the other members of your group. Listen attentively when they speak and be affirming whenever you can. This will encourage

more hesitant members of the group to participate. Always remember to show respect toward the others even if they don't always agree with your position.

5. Be careful not to dominate the discussion. By all means participate, but allow others to have equal time.

6. Try to stick to the topic being studied. There won't be enough time to handle the peripheral tough questions that come to mind during your meeting.

7. It would be helpful for you to have a good modern translation of the Bible, such as the New International Version, the New Living Translation, or the New American Standard Bible. You might prefer to use a Bible that includes notes especially for seekers, such as *The Journey: The Study Bible for Spiritual Seekers.* Unless noted otherwise, questions in this series are based on the New International Version.

8. Do some extra reading in the Bible and other recommended books as you work through these sessions. To get you started, the "Scripture for Further Study" section lists several Bible references related to each discussion, and the "Recommended Resources" section at the back of each guide offers some ideas of books to read.

## Unspeakable Love

Christianity stands or falls on Christ. Yet he left us with a whole lot of hard sayings. But the central scandal of Christianity is that at a point in history, God came down to live among us in a person, Jesus of Nazareth. And the most baffling moment of Jesus' life was on the cross, where he hung to die like a common criminal. In that place of weakness—where all seemed lost, where the taunts of "Prove yourself, Jesus, and come down from there!" lashed out like the whip that flogged him prior to his crucifixion—somehow God was at his best. There at the cross, he expressed a love greater than words could ever describe. That act of Jesus, presented as the ultimate demonstration of the love and justice of God, begs to be put to "cross" examination.

As you wrestle with these tough questions, be assured that satisfying, reasonable answers are waiting to be found. And you're invited to discover them with others in your small group as you explore and discuss these guides. God bless you on your spiritual journey!

Seek and you will find; knock and the door will be opened to you.

—Matthew 7: 7

# How Does Anyone Know God Exists?

Since the earliest of times, humankind has been incurably religious. There is a drive in the human psyche that compels us to seek out a higher power, a source for our existence, and some explanation for who we are and why we are here at all. By itself, engaging in this search is not necessarily proof that there is a God or that he can be known. But C. S. Lewis, the great English scholar and Christian philosopher, points out that even though someone's hunger is not proof that food exists or that the person will get a meal anytime soon, hunger is a powerful indicator that a person has a capacity and basic need to eat (even if he or she dies of starvation). Spiritual hunger is a powerful indicator that there is something beyond ourselves that we can—and need to—feed on. Saint Augustine expressed this longing in a prayer: "Thou has made us for Thyself, O Lord, and our hearts are restless till they rest in Thee." We all apparently have a built-in yearning to be more than just bodies and brains.

This universal quest for meaning outside ourselves is the most important journey a person can undertake. Quite literally, all other questions in life are secondary to this one. And depending on how you answer it, your life will unfold in radically different directions. If you conclude that there is no God, you will undoubtedly avoid seeking a relationship with God and build your life on principles other than God-based spiritual ones. You will not order your life trying to ascertain what God would want you to do, and you will not attempt to honor him, obey him, serve him, or in any other way submit your life to him. You will be on your own. On the other hand, if you decide he does exist and recognize that you are his creation, you will want to know everything you can about his design for you. Who are you? Why did he create you? What does he expect of you? What does he offer you? You will not want to go one minute without being in connection with him. You will want his power and his goodness to permeate your everyday life.

So this discussion guide begins with the ultimate question: "Is there a God?" There are several corollaries, such as "What is he like?" "Does he care?" and "Can I know him?" Naturally, groups of people discussing these questions will get into lively debate, which is a powerfully productive thing when accompanied by respect and honoring each other's process. I also know, as I release this guide to you, that all the mysteries of life will not become clear after just six discussions. Open minds and open Bibles will lead to great discoveries, but spiritual understanding will take time. The experience you're about to undergo will be a huge step, but probably not the last word. Even when a spiritual seeker encounters a relationship with God, he or she continues on a spiritual journey for a lifetime. *Seeking truth is a way of life, not just a season in life.*

My hope is that these sessions will facilitate animated discussion that inspires every member in your small group—no matter where each person is in his or her spiritual journey—to take one step closer to discovering the truth about who God is. I believe you will really enjoy discussing these questions. So gather some friends, neighbors, coworkers, or family members and jump in!

# Is Anybody Out There?

## *In the Beginning — God?*

Wouldn't it be great to know for sure about the existence of God?

For centuries, great minds—philosophers, theologians, and scientists—have argued various positions, hoping to settle the issue of whether or not God exists. Even today the topic is debated as intensely as ever. Sincere, intelligent people remain on all sides of the issue.

Why do some people seem so certain, while others remain skeptical? Where do you stand? If you believe he exists, how do you know? And if he doesn't, why are so many people convinced he does?

Most of us in this culture grew up hearing about God—as well as the Easter Bunny, Santa Claus, and the Tooth Fairy. Many of us said bedtime prayers. We hoped God would give us a new bike if we were good. Or we feared God's anger after stealing something from the drugstore.

Surrounded by such input since childhood, we have been ingrained with the idea of a "higher power." In fact, many people accept God as reality without even questioning. Yet as we get older, we outgrow childish dreams and fantasies. Once we learn the truth about the Easter Bunny, what do we do with God? Maybe he's the product of wishful thinking, too. Is there any evidence available for the existence of God? Or maybe

> I didn't see any God out there.
> —Yuri Gagarin, Soviet cosmonaut, after orbiting the earth

19

we shouldn't look for evidence—is God offended by people who need reasons for believing?

Often, people who have suffered greatly have the hardest time believing in God. Or at least they have trouble believing in the *goodness* of God. Norman Mailer, author of *The Gospel According to the Son,* shared this perspective: "If God is all good, then he is not all powerful. If God is all powerful, then he is not all good. I am a disbeliever in the omnipotence of God because of the Holocaust. But for thirty-five years or so, I have been believing that he is doing the best he can" (*Time,* May 5, 1997). Mailer is not an *atheist,* he's an *angry-theist.* The God of his childhood didn't fit into his adult world, so he had to redefine God— or abandon him.

What do *you* believe about the existence of God? How can you be sure? Is belief in God intellectual suicide? Tough questions . . . but worth taking the time to find answers. The purpose of these sessions is to guide you through a path of thoughtful contemplation about the existence of God and to invite you to explore and discuss all the options.

## OPEN FOR DISCUSSION

**1.** Think back to your childhood. What did you believe about God during those years? Describe a few ways your views have changed since then.

**2.** What are some factors that have influenced your current beliefs about God?

## STRAIGHT TALK

### *Positions About God*

If you were to hit the streets, survey in hand, what do you think people would say about the existence of God? Certainly you would find a wide variety of answers. Here's a summary of the positions people take with respect to the existence of God:

- The *atheist* says no god or gods exist at all. "The universe happened by chance; there is no ultimate designer."
- The *agnostic* says it is not possible to know if there is a god or not. "God may exist, but no one can know for sure."
- The *deist* says God created the universe but has left it alone ever since. "God set the world in motion like a windup toy and does not get involved."
- The *theist* says God exists and is involved with creation. "God is not only out there, he cares about his creation and desires to have a continuing active participation in it."
- The *polytheist* says many gods exist. "You have a god, I have a god, and there are many gods out there."
- The *pantheist* says that God exists in and through everything in the universe and is one with the universe. "God is part of everything; he is in the trees, in me, in you — even in that survey you're carrying."

**3.** Which of the previous positions about God represents the most common belief among people you know? Which view is least popular among your friends and acquaintances? Give reasons for your answers.

**4.** How convinced are your friends and acquaintances that their views and beliefs about God are accurate? What do you think determines the level of confidence they have?

**5.** How do you think most people decide what they're going to believe about God? On what do you think they base their beliefs about God?

**6.** Which of the views of God listed makes the most sense to you? Why?

**7.** On a scale from one to ten (one represents low confidence and ten represents high confidence), how certain are you that your view is based on actual evidence rather than opinion?

**8.** What might help to increase the level of confidence you have in what you believe about God? Explain.

An atheist is a man who believes himself an accident.

—Francis Thompson

**9.** Frequently, we place our trust (that's what *faith* means) in people or things, even though we cannot know for sure they are trustworthy—such as when we board an airplane. What other specific examples can you give of "everyday faith"?

If there were no God, there would be no atheists.

—G. K. Chesterton

**10.** During those times when absolute proof is impossible (there is no guarantee a plane will arrive safely), what factors help you determine whether you'll place your trust in something?

All I have seen teaches me to trust the Creator for all I have not seen.

—Ralph Waldo Emerson

## STRAIGHT TALK

### *Blind Faith*

Belief in God does require faith, but it does not require blind faith. You do not have to toss reason and intelligence out the window to accept the existence of God. Concluding that God exists can be a reasonable faith decision.

**11.** Since it is possible to doubt anything—and therefore impossible to prove *absolutely* the existence of God (or anything else)—what factors would help you get to reasonable certainty concerning God's existence?

## CHARTING YOUR JOURNEY

With this session you're beginning a journey. Keep in mind that you do not need to feel pressured to "say the right thing" at any point during these discussions. You're taking the time to do this work because you're looking for answers and because you're willing to be honest about your doubts and uncertainties. Others in your group would also benefit from hearing about what you'll be learning. So use these sessions profitably—ask the tough questions, think "outside the box," and learn from what others in your group have to say. But stay authentic about where you are in your journey.

To help you identify your progress more clearly, throughout this guide you will have opportunities to indicate where you are in your spiritual journey. As you gain more spiritual insights, you may find yourself reconsidering your opinions from session to session. The important thing is for you to be completely truthful about what you believe—or don't believe—right now.

**12.** Check the statement(s) below that best describes your position at this point. Share your selection with the rest of the group and give reasons for your response.

_____ There's nothing I can see that would change my opinion. I'm pretty sure there is no God—at least not the way Christians describe him.

_____ My beliefs may have been formed more by what others have taught me and not by what I really think.

_____ I think God exists, but I'm not sure I have solid reasons to back that up.

_____ I'm pretty sure God exists, but I don't know what impact that has on my life.

_____ Actually, this is an important topic. It's good to finally have a place to address questions like these.

_____ I believe God exists, and I'm hoping to learn more to understand him better.

_____ I believe God exists, but a personal opinion of this nature should be kept private.

_____ Write your own brief phrase here: _____

_____

_____

## *Scripture for Further Study*

☐ Genesis 1          ☐ Isaiah 40

☐ Job 38–41          ☐ Acts 17:11–12

☐ Psalm 14:1         ☐ Romans 1:18–32

☐ Psalm 19           ☐ 1 John 1

# How Can Anyone Be Sure God Exists?

## *Beyond Reasonable Doubt?*

Our senses are very important to us. They give us valuable information about the real world.

Think of the common experience of driving a car. Because of sight, we see the road and avoid other cars. Because of touch, we feel the steering wheel and can press the brake pedal. Because of hearing, we know, even before we see it, that an emergency vehicle is somewhere in the vicinity, so we slow down. Because of taste and smell, we enjoy the triple cheeseburger deluxe from the drive-through. In short, our senses provide for our needs and protect us from danger.

Many things aren't available to our world of five senses, yet we are dependent on those realities. We cannot see microwaves, but they cook our food. Likewise, we cannot perceive television and radio waves without specialized receivers. Even something as basic as love is impossible to touch, taste, see, smell, or hear—but who denies love exists or that it is necessary to human survival?

God also eludes our five senses. We can't see him with our eyes and we can't reach out and touch him with our hands. For some, God's failure to show up in the realm of touch, taste, sight, smell, or hearing is enough to settle the issue. "He doesn't exist," they say, "if I can't verify him with my senses." Many people, however, recognize this as probably jumping to conclusions. Maybe

> God is dead.
>
> —Friedrich Nietzsche,
> German philosopher

there are other ways to perceive what is real besides through our senses. What if we could gain information about God through intuition? What if we had a sense yet undeveloped—like a spiritual sense? And what if known abilities such as our capacity for reason could be used in our search for reliable information about God?

Consider how we piece together information and draw conclusions in the legal world. Nobody attempts to prove guilt or innocence "beyond a shadow of a doubt." Instead, we make judgments, based on evidence, "beyond a reasonable doubt." Unlike mathematical proofs, nothing in the realm of experience can be proved with absolute certainty—even an atheist will grant that. In the legal world, we talk of reasonable doubt and reasonable certainty. As long as we are human, with all our limitations, this level of confidence will have to do. And when it comes to being sure of God, it's also what we must strive for. We cannot prove God's existence beyond all possible doubt. But we can look at the "preponderance of the evidence"— and end up with reasonable certainty about God.

In this session we'll attempt to look at both sides of the argument. Like a member of a jury, you will weigh the evidence so you can begin to draw an informed conclusion that answers *reasonable* doubt.

Nietzsche and I are about to have a long talk.

—God, on the day
Nietzsche died

## OPEN FOR DISCUSSION

**1.** Give an example or two of something you place your trust in even though you are unable to perceive it with your five senses.

I do not believe in God because I don't believe in Mother Goose.

—Clarence Darrow

**2.** What is one thing you no longer believe today that you believed when you were younger? What changed your mind?

**3.** Share some of the concrete reasons you have now for your belief—or disbelief—in the existence of God.

**4.** Do you believe the sun will rise tomorrow? Why or why not? Can you provide proof for your response?

Proof is only applicable to very rarefied areas of philosophy and mathematics.... For the most part we are driven to acting on good evidence, without the luxury of proof. There is good evidence of the link between cause and effect. There is good evidence that the sun will rise tomorrow. There is good reason to believe that I am the same man as I was ten years ago. There is good reason to believe my mother loves me and is not just fattening me up for the moment when she will pop arsenic into my tea. And there is good reason to believe in God. Very good reason. Not conclusive proof, but very good reason just the same.... I believe it is much harder to reject the existence of a supreme being than accept it.

—Michael Green, *Faith for the Non-religious*

**5.** Proving something using the scientific method requires that the occurrence be repeatable (that is, somebody else has to be able to check your findings and duplicate them in their lab). It is not possible, therefore, to use the scientific method to prove or disprove the existence of God. How does this reality impact your ability or inability to believe in God?

## STRAIGHT TALK

### *Arguments Against the Existence of God*

God, were he all-powerful and perfectly good, would have created a world in which there was no unnecessary evil. . . . It has been contended that there is evil in this world—unnecessary evil—and that the more popular and philosophically more significant of the many attempts to explain this evil are completely unsatisfactory. Hence we must conclude from the existence of evil that there cannot be an omnipotent, benevolent God.

—J. McCloskey, *God and Evil*

*Self-creation.* The universe came into being spontaneously (with no known causal agent); quantum motion and combinations of space, time, and chance—not God—eventually produced the structures we observe in the universe today; everything we see can be explained in terms of known processes; therefore, there is no need to postulate a supreme deity because, in terms of the observable universe, there is nothing required for him to do.

*Spontaneous generation.* Life came about through a series of natural forces working together without the assistance of a supreme being; changes that have occurred in living beings over time give stronger evidence of evolution than of creation.

*The presence of evil.* The existence of evil in the world implies that a loving and all-powerful God cannot exist.

**6.** What arguments other than the ones on the previous page might people give against the existence of God?

**7.** To what extent do these arguments and other factors influence your own thinking that God may not exist? Explain.

## STRAIGHT TALK

### *Arguments For the Existence of God*

*Cosmological.* The fact that there is *something* (rather than nothing at all) needs an explanation. There must be a cause behind a corresponding effect; the universe is an effect, so something must have caused it. By definition, God is not an effect — he's eternal. Matter does not display this quality but rather is dependent, changeable, and, according to the current scientific theories, had a beginning (the Big Bang).

> Since the creation of the world God's invisible qualities — his eternal power and divine nature — have been clearly seen, being understood from what has been made, so that men are without excuse.
>
> — Romans 1:20

*Teleological.* The complex nature of the universe implies that there must have been a designer behind its structure. If you have a watch, there has to be a watchmaker. If there's order (and the universe does show purpose and design), there must be an order maker.

> The heavens declare the glory of God; the skies proclaim the work of his hands. Day after day they pour forth speech; night after night they display knowledge. There is no speech or language where their voice is not heard. Their voice goes out into all the earth, their words to the ends of the world.
>
> —Psalm 19:1–4

*Moral.* All people seem to have a conscience that sends signals of right and wrong. The exact standard may vary from culture to culture, but generalizations can be made that transcend all cultures. A moral creator, who put this standard in all humans, best explains the universality of this trait. "The moment you say one set of moral ideas can be better than another, you are, in fact, measuring them both by a standard, saying that one of them conforms to that standard more nearly than the other. . . . You are, in fact, comparing them both with some Real Morality, admitting that there is such a thing as a real Right, independent of what people think, and that some people's ideas get nearer to that real Right than others" (C. S. Lewis, *Mere Christianity*).

> What may be known about God is plain to them, because God has made it plain to them. . . . When Gentiles, who do not have the law, do by nature things required by the law . . . they show that the requirements of the law are written on their hearts, their consciences also bearing witness.
>
> —Romans 1:19; 2:14–15

*Experiential.* Lots of otherwise rational, reasonable people believe in God and claim he answers their prayers, guides them, and comforts them in times of need. They claim he has changed their lives, given them hope, made a difference in their values, and radically altered their behavior toward fellow human beings.

> If anyone is in Christ, he is a new creation; the old has gone, the new has come!
>
> —2 Corinthians 5:17

**8.** From the list just mentioned (or others you come up with), select the argument that for you is the strongest support of the existence of God. Which is the weakest argument? Give reasons for your selections.

**9.** Do you think most people consider the above arguments (for and against) when drawing a conclusion about the existence of God? Why or why not? Should they?

STRAIGHT TALK

### *Doubting Thomas Finds Proof*

In spite of all the philosophical arguments for the existence of God, people still have doubts. It is difficult to be convinced to the very core of your being with just these simple arguments alone. Even if you recognize that God possibly — or even probably — exists, it still may be hard to believe he does.

It's important to realize that you aren't the first one to have doubts. The Bible is full of stories of people who questioned God in one way or another. It also tells how God responds to doubters. Probably the most famous "hard sell" was Thomas, one of Jesus' close companions. He came to be called Doubting Thomas because of his skeptical response to the claim that Jesus was alive again after being dead for three days. Thomas said he wouldn't be able to believe in Jesus' resurrection — even though he readily acknowledged that the tomb was empty — unless he could actually touch Jesus and feel the wounds left from the crucifixion. He wanted sensory proof that Jesus had risen from the dead.

Jesus, without shaming Thomas, did show up, and he spoke to him: "'Put your finger here; see my hands. Reach out your hand and put it into my side. Stop doubting and believe.' Thomas said to him, 'My Lord and my God!' Then Jesus told him, 'Because you have seen me, you have believed; blessed are those who have not seen and yet have believed'" (John 20:27–29).

Notice the curious mixture in Jesus' words. While he seems very understanding of Thomas's doubts, his words have a firmness to them. He seems to think Thomas had enough evidence without the need for proof. Remember, Jesus had predicted his resurrection — and Thomas had heard those predictions. There was the empty tomb. And other people had seen Jesus alive — reliable witnesses whom Thomas knew. So Thomas's disbelief was a matter more of his will than of lack of evidence. A rebuke was not entirely out of order.

Yet the bottom line is that Jesus met Thomas at his point of need. And Jesus promises a blessing to the many others — all the rest of us down through the ages — who will come to believe in him based on the historical evidence God provided.

## HEART OF THE MATTER

**10.** Why do you think Jesus said that people who do not see and yet still believe will be blessed?

**11.** There probably isn't a person alive who hasn't had doubts about the existence of God. When have you experienced these doubts, and how have you dealt with them?

**12.** Let's assume you have had, or currently have, doubts about God. If you are willing, try this experiment on your own. Ask God to make himself real to you. Ask him to show you, in ways that will be meaningful to you, that he can be relied upon. Does this experiment seem reasonable to you? Is this something you would be open to trying sometime? Why or why not?

## STRAIGHT TALK

### *Afraid to Believe?*

Notice that believing in God is more than just an intellectual exercise. Our emotions get involved. When we make a request of God (such as the one outlined in question 12), what we're really asking is not merely, "God, show me if you're there." We want to know if he *cares.* We want to know if we're important to him — important enough that he would reach into our experience, into our lives, and make a connection.

In addition to God's existence, we need to know about his character. After all, if God does exist but is some kind of monster, who would want to relate to him? For some reason, most of us seem to be afraid of God. We have preconceived ideas about him that scare us away, and our fears can influence the very reasoning ability we need to readily observe the evidence in order to believe in him.

Our personal concept of God—when we pray, for instance—is worthless unless it coincides with his revelation of himself.

—Paul E. Little,
*Know What You Believe*

**13.** What are your fears about God and what he might be like? How do you think those fears affect your confidence in his existence, or your ability to trust him?

## CHARTING YOUR JOURNEY

**14.** Check the statement(s) below that best describes your position at this point. Share your selection with the rest of the group and give reasons for your response.

_____ I'm still pretty sure there is no God—at least the way Christians describe him.

_____ I'm open to looking for evidence but doubtful it will change my mind.

_____ I think God exists, but I'm not sure I have solid reasons to back that up.

_____ I'm pretty sure God exists, but I don't know what impact that has on my life.

_____ These discussions are helping me to grow my confidence in God.

_____ I need to make a relationship with God a greater priority in my life.

_____ I believe God exists, and I'm hoping to learn more to understand him better.

_____ I believe God exists, but a personal opinion of this nature should be kept private.

_____ Write your own brief phrase here: _____

_____

_____

## Scripture for Further Study

- ☐ Exodus 34
- ☐ Job 38–41
- ☐ Jeremiah 23:29
- ☐ Mark 4:36–41
- ☐ 2 Corinthians 5:7
- ☐ Hebrews 2:1–4
- ☐ Hebrews 4:12
- ☐ Hebrews 11:1–3

# What Is God Really Like?

## *Nice to Meet You?*

Imagine you were going to have dinner with the president of your company. If that person had a reputation for being a loud-mouthed tyrant, insensitive to anybody's feelings but his own, you would probably not look forward to the meal. But if he was kind, thoughtful, and took a personal interest in everyone in the company, you'd probably be eager to meet with him. The desire you have to get to know the president is greatly influenced by what you think he's really like—not necessarily the position he has in the company.

The same may be true with our view of God. Many people have little or no interest in God because of what they have heard about him or imagined him to be like. If he isn't the sort of deity they want to know on an intimate level, it doesn't matter that he's God—he's not someone they consider worth knowing.

We all have our own concept of God's nature and personality. These ideas are influenced by a wide variety of factors. For example, the way we envision God has a lot to do with what we were taught about him while we were growing up. Parents, teachers, and ministers can instill in us a concept about God with such indelibility, it can last a lifetime. There's also a strong tendency for us to view God the way we view our parents. How our parents treated us while we were growing up influences to some degree our assumptions of how God might treat us now. (In his book *Your God Is Too Small,* J. B. Phillips called this phenomenon "parental hangover.")

If we understand God as a person and not just a force, we will tend to view him in the likeness of people we know—and the intensity of our desire to know him personally rises or falls depending on the desirability of that picture. Our images of God most likely fit into three general, personal categories. Some picture God as a kindhearted grandfather—a simple old guy who smiles and laughs and delights to give good gifts to his loved ones. Others see God as a stern police officer—a strict and sometimes mean killjoy who has a long list of rules that must be enforced. And there are those who imagine God to be a cosmic mechanic—a repairman whose purpose is to fix life's problems when called upon for help.

Although we know these are just stereotypes, which comes closest to the real God? Does the Bible present a unified picture of what he's like? How willing are any of us to give up our preconceptions and come to know the God who is actually there?

These are very important questions because coming to a belief in God is more than just acknowledging a supreme being. If our view of God is too far off, we will be in danger of something the Bible calls idolatry. We will be worshiping a god in our image instead of relating to the God who made us in his image. So it's not just an academic issue. To believe in God, according to Christianity, is to enter into a relationship with him. And to have that relationship, we must know who he is—and what he is really like.

What we believe about God is the most important thing about us.

—A. W. Tozer

**1.** Imagine you are taking a survey, asking people what they think God is like. What are the most common characteristics they would mention?

**2.** Which of the three images of God mentioned in the introduction (grandfather, policeman, mechanic) most closely resembles your own understanding of God? What circumstances in your past have contributed to that image of him?

## STRAIGHT TALK

### *Attributes of God*

The Bible describes God with a variety of pictures, symbols, and words. Taken together, a consistent and fully orbed picture emerges. Theologians refer to the term *attributes* when enumerating the characteristics of God. The following list explains in simple terms those attributes and their meanings.

> Because God has spoken and has revealed himself, we no longer have the need or the option of conjuring up ideas and images of God by our own imaginations.
>
> —Paul E. Little

### Ways We Cannot Attempt to Imitate Him

*Omnipresent.* He is always near; no place is farther from him than any other place; he is not limited to any spatial dimensions.

*Omnipotent.* He can do anything that doesn't violate his nature; he's all-powerful; nothing is impossible for him; his power is unlimited and unrestricted except by his own choice.

*Omniscient.* He knows everything; nothing is hidden; nothing goes unnoticed; no situation or possible scenario is beyond his ability to grasp; all mysteries are clear to him; no one can tell him something he doesn't already know.

*Sovereign.* He is the ultimate ruler of the universe; no one has greater authority or power than he; no sin or disobedience can thwart the purposes he desires to bring to pass.

*Eternal.* He always has been; he always will be; he had no beginning; he'll have no end; he is the creator of time; he is not subject to time but rules over it.

*Immutable.* He doesn't change; he isn't getting better; his attributes can't be diminished; he doesn't grow or increase; he's perfect the way he is, and we can rest assured he will continue that way.

*Infinite.* He is unlimited; whatever he is, he is that to an infinite degree; you can't measure any part of him or his attributes; he is inexhaustible in every aspect of his being.

### Ways We Can Attempt to Imitate Him

*Holy.* He's pure; he's morally perfect and without fault; he can't be compared with anyone or anything, because he's so much more virtuous than everything we've known or experienced.

*Wise.* He uses his knowledge skillfully; he makes sense; he has tremendous insight; his counsel can be trusted.

*Good.* He has no evil, can do no evil; he works for the benefit of his creatures; he can be trusted with our well-being.

*Just.* He is fair; he doesn't tolerate unrighteousness; he will make sure every wrong will be made right; he is impartial.

*Loving.* Sacrifice is in his very nature; he cares; he gives; he serves; he works to bring about what we need; he's compassionate; he's sensitive; he chooses to hold us in high regard; we matter to him.

**3.** Which of the attributes listed grab your attention more than the others? Explain why those characteristics stand out for you.

**4.** As you examine the list, are there any attributes that surprise or confuse you? Which ones and why?

**5.** Given the list of God's attributes, does God seem appealing to you? Why or why not? To what degree would you like to get to know God better?

I do not trouble myself with the possibility that God may exist after all. If he exists (which seems to me more than doubtful), I am in for a bad time in the next world, but I am not going to bargain to believe in God in order to save my soul. Pascal's wager— the bet he took with himself that God existed, even though this could not be proved by reasoning—strikes me too prudential. What had Pascal to lose by behaving as if he existed? Absolutely nothing, for there was no counter-Principle to damn him in case God didn't. For myself, I prefer not to play it so safe, and I shall never send for a priest or recite an Act of Contrition in my last moments. I do not mind if I lose my soul for all eternity. If the kind of God exists who would damn me for not working out a deal with him, then that is unfortunate. I should not care to spend eternity in the company of such a person.

—Mary McCarthy

**6.** You've probably heard someone say, "My God is not like that at all—my God is _____ _____," inserting words like "more loving," "less judgmental," "a forgiving God," "not old-fashioned," or something else. Fill in this blank with words you've heard or said yourself. What's your reaction to the thinking behind such statements?

We are more at home with our own ideas about religion—with thoughts which are more comfortable and reassuring, with a "God" who is rather like us and who can be brought into line with our own expectations. This God is domesticated—like a religious "pet," rather than the wild, untamed presence of the Almighty.

—David Hewetson and David Miller, *Christianity Made Simple*

**7.** Comment on the following statement: "Our opinions of God are like feathers caught in a gust, which can neither alter nor redirect the force of the wind. Our task is to discover God's true nature—to see what he's shown us about himself—regardless of our preferences." Do you agree with this statement? Why or why not?

**8.** Select one of the attributes listed earlier in the session. Take a few minutes to silently think about what it would mean to you personally if God truly had that attribute. Picture your daily life being affected by that characteristic of God. Now, using the spokes of the wheel below, explain what your life could be like if you really accepted God for all that he is and allowed him to demonstrate that attribute toward you in each area of your life.

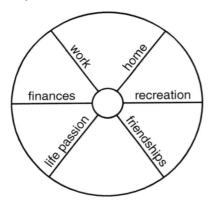

**9.** The Bible says in James 2:19 that even the devil believes in God and trembles. What do you suppose is missing from the devil's position about God? How is it possible to believe intellectually that God exists but then live as though he does not exist?

**10.** Expand on what you think is meant by the following statement: "It's one thing to believe that the God described in the Bible exists, and quite another to let that belief impact your life." Do you agree with this statement? Why or why not?

**11.** What is your greatest fear about what you'd be like and the changes that would take place if God were leading your life?

## CHARTING YOUR JOURNEY

**12.** Check the statement(s) below that best describes your position at this point. Share your selection with the rest of the group and give reasons for your response.

_____ I'm not sure I believe that the way the Bible describes God is really accurate.

_____ My concept of God is somewhat different from the God depicted in this lesson.

_____ I'm open to thinking about God in new ways.

_____ I'm still not sure what I believe and don't believe about God.

_____ The Bible is my supreme source for authoritative information about God, and I'd like to learn more about him.

_____ I know a lot about God, but it is not affecting my life as much as it should.

_____ Write your own brief phrase here: _____

_____

_____

## Scripture for Further Study

☐ 2 Chronicles 19:7 ☐ Luke 15

☐ Isaiah 40 ☐ John 4:24

☐ Isaiah 46:5, 9 ☐ John 17:3

☐ Psalm 57:10 ☐ Ephesians 1:19–23

☐ Matthew 15:8–9 ☐ Hebrews 1

☐ Matthew 19:17

# How Can Rational People Believe in Miracles?

## It's a Miracle?

A college student gets a passing grade on a final exam and shouts, "It's a miracle!" A girl accepts her heart-throb's surprise invitation to go out on a date and hangs up the phone sighing, "Miracles do happen!" A husband bursts through the door after driving an hour with the gas gauge on empty and exclaims to his wife, "It's a miracle I got home!"

If that's what we mean by *miracle,* then who could deny that miracles happen? Life is full of pleasant surprises and long shots that come through. But a miracle, in the biblical sense, is an intervention in the natural world by the power of God. A miracle is something God does that appears to defy the laws of nature. It is a *super*natural act.

The God of the Bible is a miracle-working God. He not only made the world, but he also rearranges parts of it from time to time. At least that's the claim. Yet thinking people can't help wonder: Did all those stories in the Bible really happen? Who believes anymore that a flood killed all the inhabitants of the world except for Noah and those in the ark? Did Moses really part the Red Sea? What about all those healings Jesus supposedly performed? And the real topper—

Children are not born to virgins, angels do not bring messages to people, men do not walk on water, people who die do not return to life, and so on. The story of Jesus Christ was filled with what men had learned were impossibilities; therefore, the story could not be a literal account of actual happenings. When the New Testament was written, men may have been naïve enough to believe the things that were said about Jesus, and they may have seen no contradiction between the reports and their knowledge of the world, but now all was otherwise.

—*Protestantism,* as cited in *Answers to Tough Questions* by Josh McDowell

Jesus rising from the dead? Surely all these fantastic stories in the Bible are just that—stories, which were never meant to be taken literally.

It's natural to suppose that accounts of miracles are nothing more than exaggerations. Well-intended people were amazed by an event, and after many retellings, their stories grew into an act of God. We see this kind of thing all the time as stories are passed from person to person. Besides, long ago people weren't as educated as we are now. They tended to attribute perfectly natural phenomena (for example, lightning) to the power of the gods (in this case, the Greek god Zeus). Given such an unsophisticated, pre-scientific environment, it's no wonder people were easily fooled into thinking that blind men received sight or that loaves and fishes suddenly multiplied out of thin air.

A further objection can be raised. If we are to take all these miracle stories literally, why don't we see similar things happening today? When was the last time you heard of anyone walking on water? Why haven't any reporters interviewed a three-days-dead man now alive again? Supposedly, these were acts of God. Is he tired now? Has he gotten out of the miracle business?

It is undeniable that the Bible claims miracles happened. Christianity without miracles is nothing more than a list of how-tos for being a better person—with no power to become one and no forgiveness when you're not. So if miracles don't occur, if the reports in the Bible are either exaggerations, simple-minded stories, or—worse—outright deception, if God doesn't exist, or if he does exist but didn't do the things attributed to him, hear this clearly: *Christianity is not true.* It is a false religion and should be discarded as a pious fraud.

This session cannot look at every miracle in the Bible and prove each one beyond reasonable doubt. What is worth looking at is the possibility of miracles. So it does

All the essentials of Hinduism would, I think, remain unimpaired if you subtracted the miraculous, and the same is almost true of Muhammedanism, but you cannot do that with Christianity. It is precisely the story of a great miracle. A naturalistic Christianity leaves out all that is specifically Christian.

—C. S. Lewis

address the question "Could miracles occur?" As you'll see, ruling out miracles before you've even looked at the evidence is irrational—much more so than at least being open to their plausibility.

1. Consider the following list of events: a spectacular sunset, the birth of a baby, the healing of a broken bone, a complete recovery from cancer without medical treatment, and a man walking on water. Which of these events would you label as a miracle? Why?

It is impossible to use electrical light and the wireless and to avail ourselves of modern medical and surgical discoveries, and at the same time to believe in the New Testament world of spirits and miracles.

—Rudolf Bultmann

2. Why do you suppose many people find it difficult, if not impossible, to believe in miracles?

Nothing can happen without cause; nothing happens that cannot happen, and when what was capable of happening has happened, it may not be interpreted as a miracle. Consequently, there are no miracles ... We therefore draw this conclusion: what was capable of happening is not a miracle.

—Cicero, *De Divinatione,* 2.28

## Do Miracles Contradict the Laws of Nature?

For the purposes of this discussion, the term *miracle* will be defined as "an event that cannot be given a natural explanation but must be attributed directly to God, who has acted in a special way in the natural order" (C. Stephen Evans, *Why Believe?*).

Ken Boa and Larry Moody, in their book *I'm Glad You Asked,* state, "If you took a flying leap off the edge of a sheer cliff, the natural law of gravity would cause you to face dire consequences; but if you were to take another leap off the same cliff in a hang glider, the results would (hopefully!) be quite different. To claim that miracles violate or contradict natural laws is just as improper as to say that the principle of aerodynamics violates the law of gravity."

This is an important concept to keep in mind when it is argued, "If something happens, it can happen; therefore, if it can happen, by definition it's not a miracle." When God exercises his power, he acts on the natural world—it is his power working on molecules, atoms, photons, etc. A miracle has its source in God, even though its effects are in nature. God uses nature and natural laws to create a miracle, but he's doing so directly instead of having the laws of physics he set in place cause the effect.

In the example above, the hang glider doesn't cancel gravity; it just uses the aerodynamic force of lift to counteract the gravity that is still in force. If you were miraculously suspended in air, gravity would still be operative on you—but God would be exercising his power to counteract the gravity attracting you to the earth. Therefore a miracle is something that can happen only if God is at work in that circumstance. It couldn't happen if God chose to remove his power. The whole thing hinges on whether or not God is involved, not whether something can or cannot happen.

Behind this important question [about miracles] is the familiar issue of whether or not God exists. For if there is a God, then certainly miracles are possible. In fact, the very nature of the question: "How are miracles possible?" presupposes there is a God, for a miracle is an act of God.

—Josh McDowell,
*Answers to Tough Questions*

**3.** What do you think of the following statement: "If God doesn't exist, by definition miracles don't happen, because a miracle is an act of God. If, on the other hand, God does exist and he is the creator of the universe, miracles are possible because the God who created everything has the power to choose to do something else."

There are two ways to look at life. One is that nothing is a miracle, and the other is that everything is a miracle.

—Albert Einstein

## STRAIGHT TALK

### *Examining Miracles*

Just because miracles are *possible* does not necessarily mean they have actually occurred — and certainly everything claimed to be miraculous is not. The evidence for any miracle — and biblical miracles in particular — comes from an examination of the event. The first question is "Did the event occur?" The next question is "Did the event occur because God acted?" These are not theological questions; they are historical ones.

Take, for example, how the apostle Paul talks about the miracle of the resurrection of Jesus. He points out the seriousness of the event: "If Christ has not been raised, our preaching is useless and so is your faith" (1 Corinthians 15:14). One key historical datum to consider regarding the resurrection is the substantiation of an empty tomb. If Jesus' tomb was in fact empty, there are two possibilities: either the body was moved or the body was resurrected. Paul cites evidence for the resurrection as a matter of history, not opinion or wish fulfillment:

> What I received I passed on to you as of first importance: that Christ died for our sins according to the Scriptures, that he

was buried, that he was raised on the third day according to the Scriptures, and that he appeared to Peter, and then to the Twelve. After that, he appeared to more than five hundred of the brothers at the same time, most of whom are still living, though some have fallen asleep. Then he appeared to James, then to all the apostles, and last of all he appeared to me also, as to one abnormally born.

—1 Corinthians 15:3–8

**4.** Why would Paul make a point of noting the eyewitnesses who saw Jesus back from the dead? Why would the mention of five hundred people who simultaneously saw Jesus be a powerful piece of evidence?

[Those who hold that miracles are not possible assert that] the universe operates according to uniform natural causes, and that it is impossible for any force outside the universe to intervene in the cosmos. This, of course, is an anti-supernatural assumption that only atheists can hold consistently.

—Ken Boa and Larry Moody, *I'm Glad You Asked*

## STRAIGHT TALK

### *The Purpose of Miracles*

Consider the purpose of miracles. John 2:23 says, "While he was in Jerusalem at the Passover Feast, many people saw the miraculous signs he was doing and believed in his name." John 10:24–25 says, "The Jews gathered around him, saying, 'How long will you keep us in suspense? If you are the Christ, tell us plainly.' Jesus answered, 'I did tell you, but you do not believe. The miracles I do in my Father's name speak for me.'"

**5.** According to these passages, what is the value of Jesus' miracles? Even though we are twenty centuries removed from the events, how is his point still valid?

The miracles of the Bible are firmly embedded in space-time history, and the truth of Christianity stands or falls with the historicity of these miracles, especially the Resurrection. Passages such as John 10:25, John 14:11, John 15:24 and 1 Corinthians 15:12–19 underscore the centrality of miracles to the truth claims of Christianity.

—Ken Boa and Larry Moody, *I'm Glad You Asked*

## HEART OF THE MATTER

**6.** Have you ever had a personal experience that you believe to be a miracle? Tell your group about that experience.

**7.** What is your emotional reaction to the thought that God might do something in your life that you couldn't explain? What about the idea that he could do something miraculous for you, but hasn't?

## Who's Behind the Miracles?

Even Jesus' enemies admitted he performed miracles — an important point for modern skeptics to note. They stubbornly refused to follow him, however, attributing his power to evil — to the devil: "When the Pharisees heard this, they said, 'It is only by Beelzebub, the prince of demons, that this fellow drives out demons'" (Matthew 12:24). The Pharisees didn't deny that the events occurred; they just said it wasn't God's power that made it happen.

**8.** What insight can you gain into human nature (and the limits of a miracle's ability to convince a biased heart) from this irrational reaction to Jesus' miracles?

**9.** What specific questions about Christianity have you struggled with (in the past or now) that relate to the issue of miracles?

**10.** Do you agree with the statement "If miracles never happen, Christianity cannot be true"? Explain.

**11.** Check the statement(s) below that best describes your position at this point. Share your selection with the rest of the group and give reasons for your response.

_____ I really can't believe miracles have ever occurred.

_____ I'm open to evidence about miracles.

_____ I'd have to see a miracle with my own eyes to believe in one.

_____ I hope the miracles in the Bible occurred even if I don't have any proof.

_____ I'm not sure what two-thousand-year-old miracles have to do with life here and now.

_____ I'm convinced the miracles in the Bible are real.

_____ Write your own brief phrase here: _____

_____

_____

## Scripture for Further Study

- ☐ Genesis 18:14
- ☐ 1 Chronicles 29:10–13
- ☐ Jeremiah 32:17–21, 26–27
- ☐ Matthew 8:23–27
- ☐ Luke 24

- ☐ John 2:1–11
- ☐ John 11
- ☐ John 12:27–30
- ☐ Acts 1:1–11
- ☐ Ephesians 1:19–23
- ☐ 1 Peter 3:22

# Does God Care about What Happens to Us?

## *Just a Speck?*

Imagine yourself in an airplane flying high above where you're sitting, looking down from thirty-five thousand feet. Roads and buildings appear very small from this distance. Now go higher than the plane—way higher—and picture yourself in space, seeing the earth below. Go farther still, zooming out until the sun and all the planets of our solar system are in the picture. As your mental camera keeps ascending into the vast, dark, mysterious realm of the universe, our whole solar system becomes merely a speck in a misty blanket of stars that form our galaxy. Beyond that, our galaxy is only one among billions of other galaxies, all racing away from each other at mind-boggling speeds.

As you contemplate the vastness of the cosmos, it's hard to find much significance in one human life. How could any one of us really matter in the eternal scheme of things? Even if there is a God who created all this, why should such a powerful being care about a fleck of respiring carbon on a small, water-covered rock circling an average star among billions and billions of others? Only the most naive, self-centered child could think he or she really had a place of significance in the world, let alone before such a majestic being.

It's not just the size of everything that makes us seem insignificant. How many billions of people have come before us? How many billions will follow before the sun burns out and the earth is left a charred, cold cinder? With all these other lives to pay attention to, how could God invest any one of us with significance? And look at all the apparent randomness in human history. How can anyone say there's some kind of plan unfolding, let alone a plan that encompasses each of us and allows for our unique contribution?

You are not alone if you've had such thoughts. Even if we grant that God exists, the chance that we matter to him would seem slim to none. Edward K. Boyd, describing his view of this dilemma in *Letters from a Skeptic,* writes,

> I have trouble with the whole idea of talking to God so long as I am nagged with the idea that we aren't central, or even important, to anything he's doing. I grant that the almighty force behind the creation has personal characteristics, but I'm still not convinced that this has any bearing on us. His agenda seems to be with something else in the universe. It seems to me that we are an accidental feature to the whole thing. Why would God suffer for creatures as insignificant as us? I could see how people believed this back in the Middle Ages when they thought the earth was the center of everything. But we now know that the earth is this little insignificant planet, in a relatively small solar system, in a relatively small galaxy, which is located nowhere in particular in an incomprehensibly large universe. So what's the big deal with us? Why couldn't it be that he has a purpose for the universe, but we are simply not part of it? Is there anything to suggest that we are that important, or important at all?

We are, undeniably, mere specks in the eye of the universe. Can it possibly be, as Christianity claims, that we are also cherished children of a heavenly Father? Is there any evidence that God—if he exists— cares about us?

The universe we observe has precisely the properties we should expect if there is, at bottom, no design, no purpose, no evil, and no good, nothing but blind, pitiless indifference.

—Richard Dawkins, *River Out of Eden*

**1.** Describe a situation in which you misplaced or lost something very valuable. What did you do? How did that loss make you feel? How did you react when you finally discovered the valuable item for which you were looking? (If you never did find it, how did you react when you finally realized it was gone forever?)

**2.** To what extent do you feel God cares about you and your life? Explain.

## STRAIGHT TALK

### The Lost Sheep

One of the ways Jesus taught was to use interesting stories (called parables) that drove home a strong point. Look at the following story.

> The tax collectors and "sinners" were all gathering around to hear him. But the Pharisees and the teachers of the law

muttered, "This man welcomes sinners and eats with them." Then Jesus told them this parable: "Suppose one of you has a hundred sheep and loses one of them. Does he not leave the ninety-nine in the open country and go after the lost sheep until he finds it? And when he finds it, he joyfully puts it on his shoulders and goes home. Then he calls his friends and neighbors together and says, 'Rejoice with me; I have found my lost sheep.' I tell you that in the same way there will be more rejoicing in heaven over one sinner who repents than over ninety-nine righteous persons who do not need to repent."

— Luke 15:1–7

**3.** What attitude is Jesus responding to when he begins to tell this parable?

## STRAIGHT TALK

### *The Lost Coin*

Jesus then told the following parable:

Suppose a woman has ten silver coins and loses one. Does she not light a lamp, sweep the house and search carefully until she finds it? And when she finds it, she calls her friends and neighbors together and says, "Rejoice with me; I have found my lost coin." In the same way, I tell you, there is rejoicing in the presence of the angels of God over one sinner who repents.

— Luke 15:8–10

**4.** Do you suppose this woman was greedy? What additional motive could have been behind her frantic search?

### The Lost Son

Jesus continued:

There was a man who had two sons. The younger one said to his father, "Father, give me my share of the estate." So he divided his property between them.

Not long after that, the younger son got together all he had, set off for a distant country and there squandered his wealth in wild living. After he had spent everything, there was a severe famine in that whole country, and he began to be in need. So he went and hired himself out to a citizen of that country, who sent him to his fields to feed pigs. He longed to fill his stomach with the pods that the pigs were eating, but no one gave him anything.

When he came to his senses, he said, "How many of my father's hired men have food to spare, and here I am starving to death! I will set out and go back to my father and say to him: Father, I have sinned against heaven and against you. I am no longer worthy to be called your son; make me like one of your hired men." So he got up and went to his father.

But while he was still a long way off, his father saw him and was filled with compassion for him; he ran to his son, threw his arms around him and kissed him.

The son said to him, "Father, I have sinned against heaven and against you. I am no longer worthy to be called your son."

But the father said to his servants, "Quick! Bring the best robe and put it on him. Put a ring on his finger and sandals on his feet. Bring the fattened calf and kill it. Let's have a feast and celebrate. For this son of mine was dead and is alive again; he was lost and is found." So they began to celebrate.

— Luke 15:11–24

**5.** The two main elements in each parable symbolize the same two things. What is the common thread that binds these parables together? In other words, what do you suppose the two main elements in each parable represent?

- parable 1 elements: shepherd and sheep

- parable 2 elements: woman and coins

- parable 3 elements: father and son

    A. The first element (shepherd, woman, and father) represents _____.

    B. The second element (sheep, coins, and son) represents _____.

**6.** Describe the reaction common to all three stories when the missing valuable was finally found.

**7.** According to Jesus, what do these three stories teach concerning how much God values lost people? How then would you suppose God reacts when lost people come to him?

**8.** Think back to your description of how you felt when you lost something very valuable. How does your reaction in that situation compare with how God must feel toward those who are not yet part of his family?

You can cite a hundred references to show that the biblical God is a bloodthirsty tyrant, but if they can dig up two or three verses that say, "God is love," they will claim that you are taking things out of context!

—Dan Barker,
*Losing Faith in Faith*

**9.** How do you feel about the idea that God hosts a heavenly celebration when a single person like you comes to him and is found?

**10.** Read Matthew 6:25–26 and Matthew 10:29–31. What points in these verses are easy for you to accept? What points are difficult for you to agree with?

**11.** How difficult is it for you to really sense God's love for you personally? What factors influence this ability? Describe times in your life when you have felt loved by God.

**12.** What would God need to do in order for you to feel loved by him? What is your understanding of what he has done already?

**13.** On a scale from one to ten, place an *X* near the spot and phrase that best describes you. Share your selection with the rest of the group and give reasons for placing your *X* where you did.

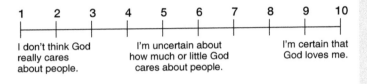

```
1    2    3    4    5    6    7    8    9    10
├────┼────┼────┼────┼────┼────┼────┼────┼────┤
```

I don't think God
really cares
about people.

I'm uncertain about
how much or little God
cares about people.

I'm certain that
God loves me.

### Scripture for Further Study

- ☐ Genesis 12:1–3
- ☐ Genesis 15
- ☐ Psalm 19
- ☐ Psalm 23
- ☐ Psalm 33:13–22
- ☐ Psalm 34:15
- ☐ Psalm 57:10
- ☐ Psalm 139
- ☐ Isaiah 41:10, 13

- ☐ Isaiah 55
- ☐ Matthew 1:18–25
- ☐ Matthew 10:29–31
- ☐ Luke 1:46–56
- ☐ Ephesians 2:8–9
- ☐ Philippians 2:5–11
- ☐ 2 Peter 3:9
- ☐ Revelation 4:11

# How Can a Person Get to Know God?

## Fans or Fanatics?

Imagine two sports fans sitting next to each other at the ballpark, meeting each other for the first time. Within minutes, they're discussing their favorite professional baseball heroes, swapping stories about the times they saw these players in action. They quiz each other on all the facts and figures that highlight the players' various accomplishments.

At one point, the first fan asks the second fan, "What do you know about Hank Aaron?" The other replies, "I know a *lot* about him—he's my all-time favorite!" He goes on and on, reciting all the amazing statistics about this great home run hitter. To cap off the conversation, he slowly pulls out of his jacket pocket a treasured baseball card with Hank Aaron's picture and autograph. Holding it out proudly, he gloats, "If anyone knows Hank Aaron, it's me!" He pauses for just a minute, gazing at the baseball card, and then turns with a challenge, "So, what do *you* know about Hank Aaron?"

"Well," comes the response, "I *really* know him." The other fan chuckles with a snort. But laughter turns to shock as the first fan produces a family photo with Hank Aaron in the center, his arm around a guy with a familiar-looking face. "He's my grandfather!"

It's one thing to know a lot of facts *about* a person; it's quite a different thing to actually *know* the person—

to have a relationship with him or her. It's not the amount of information that makes the difference; it's the actual encounter.

Up to this point in this guide, we've considered a wide range of questions about God. We've discussed the existence of God and what factors influence a person's beliefs about God. We've examined some of the attributes of God—those traits that identify him as distinctly and uniquely God. We've explored the reasons people have for believing in miracles, and the issue of God's concern for us. These sessions may have helped you to *want* to know God, by clarifying who he is. But how do you *actually* begin a relationship with him? How can a person really get to know God personally and encounter him in a meaningful way? And is such a thing even possible?

## OPEN FOR DISCUSSION

**1.** Describe a situation in which you admired someone from a distance and then had an opportunity to meet and get to know the person. How did your perspective change concerning the person?

2. Do you know people who believe they have encountered God in a way that is more significant and personal than merely knowing facts about him? What do you suppose they mean by this?

3. What do you think causes the barrier that seems to exist between God and people? Read Isaiah 59:1–2. According to this passage, what causes a separation between God and us? Why does this form such an impenetrable barrier?

## STRAIGHT TALK

### Slamming the Door

It's important to keep in mind, as we seek to move toward God, that the Bible does not portray any of us in a "neutral" position with him. Every one of us needs to be reminded that contact with God has been broken from *our* side — he didn't hide; we, in effect, slammed the door in his face. We've turned our backs collectively as a human race and, more to the point, we've each done that in our individual lives.

When a person begins to pursue a relationship with God, part of what must be acknowledged is that the reason we have to seek at all is because we told God to go away. While each of us has done that in our own unique way, we have all violated two important principles: we've all failed to acknowledge God as God, based on what we observe of him in creation, and we've all failed to live up to God's standards — which we minimally understand by what our consciences tell us is right and wrong. These two shortfalls are true of every human being on the planet. Until this twofold rejection is dealt with, seeking God is only a philosophical, not a personal, journey.

**4.** Romans 5:8 says, "God demonstrates his own love for us in this: While we were still sinners, Christ died for us." What does this verse say about how God feels toward people who have shunned him and are therefore separated from him?

Surely the arm of the Lord is not too short to save, nor his ear too dull to hear. But your iniquities have separated you from your God; your sins have hidden his face from you.

—Isaiah 59:1–2

**5.** Romans 6:23 teaches, "The wages of sin is death, but the gift of God is eternal life in Christ Jesus our Lord." What is the biblical consequence associated with this gap between God and us? Expand on what that might mean in everyday life (not just at the end of life).

**6.** John 3:16–17 states, "For God so loved the world that he gave his one and only Son, that whoever believes in him shall not perish but have eternal life. For God did not send his Son into the world to condemn the world, but to save the world through him." According to these verses, what did God do to overcome the distance between people and himself?

> We were created to enjoy a special relationship with God. We were made to know and enjoy God and cannot truly fulfill our destiny apart from him. Though we need God and cannot truly be happy without him; we are usually far from understanding this. Instead, we constantly run away from God and try to replace him with substitutes.
>
> —C. Stephen Evans,
> *Why Believe?*

**7.** John 17:3 says, "This is eternal life: that they may know you, the only true God, and Jesus Christ, whom you have sent." What does Jesus say eternal life is really all about? What does it mean to "know" God and Jesus Christ?

## HEART OF THE MATTER

**8.** To what extent do you feel you need to encounter God and know him on a deep personal level?

**9.** What factors do you think influence a person to make a complete turnaround in what he or she believes spiritually?

**10.** Describe an experience in which God was very real to you (if you have had such an experience).

**11.** The verses listed in questions 5, 6, and 7 above show what the Bible teaches about getting to know God for the first time—that is, how we cross over from belief *about* God to having an intimate, permanent spiritual connection *with* God based on his offer of love and forgiveness. How does this information differ from what you have believed (now or in the past) concerning how a person can know God personally? What barriers prevent you from taking this kind of step toward God?

All of us have been created with a God-shaped vacuum that only God can fill.

—Blaise Pascal

**12.** Now that we're at the end of this discussion guide, at what point would you describe yourself to be in your spiritual journey? On a scale from one to ten, place an *X* near the spot and phrase that best describes you and where you are now. Share your selection with the rest of the group and give reasons for placing your *X* where you did.

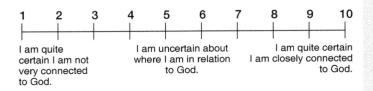

1    2    3    4    5    6    7    8    9    10

I am quite
certain I am not
very connected
to God.

I am uncertain about
where I am in relation
to God.

I am quite certain
I am closely connected
to God.

## *Scripture for Further Study*

- ☐ Isaiah 53:6
- ☐ Psalm 23
- ☐ Psalm 51
- ☐ Matthew 14:22–33
- ☐ John 10
- ☐ John 14:23–24

- ☐ Romans 10:9–18
- ☐ Galatians 1
- ☐ Hebrews 11
- ☐ 1 John 1:8–10
- ☐ 1 John 3:1
- ☐ Revelation 3:20

# Recommended Resources

Ken Boa and Larry Moody, *I'm Glad You Asked* (Chariot Victor, 1995).

Gregory Boyd and Edward Boyd, *Letters from a Skeptic* (Chariot Victor, 1994).

William Lane Craig, *Reasonable Faith* (Crossway, 1994).

C. Stephen Evans, *Why Believe?* (Eerdmans, 1996).

Cliffe Knechtle, *Give Me an Answer* (InterVarsity, 1986).

Cliffe Knechtle, *Help Me Believe* (InterVarsity, 2000).

Andrew Knowles, *Finding Faith* (Lion, 1994).

Peter Kreeft and Ronald Tacelli, *Handbook of Christian Apologetics* (InterVarsity, 1994).

C. S. Lewis, *Mere Christianity* (HarperSanFransisco, 2001).

C. S. Lewis, *Miracles* (HarperSanFransisco, 2001).

Paul Little, *Know What You Believe* (Chariot Victor, 1987).

Paul Little, *Know Why You Believe* (InterVarsity, 2000).

Lee Strobel, *The Case for Christ* (Zondervan, 1998).

Lee Strobel, *The Case for Faith* (Zondervan, 2000).

# Willow Creek Association
*Vision, Training, Resources for Prevailing Churches*

This resource was created to serve you and to help you in building a local church that prevails!

Since 1992, the Willow Creek Association (WCA) has been linking like-minded, action-oriented churches with each other and with strategic vision, training, and resources. Now a worldwide network of over 6,400 churches from more than ninety denominations, the WCA works to equip Member Churches and others with the tools needed to build prevailing churches. Our desire is to inspire, equip, and encourage Christian leaders to build biblically functioning churches that reach increasing numbers of unchurched people, not just with innovations from Willow Creek Community Church in South Barrington, Illinois, but from any church in the world that has experienced God-given breakthroughs.

## WILLOW CREEK CONFERENCES

Each year, thousands of local church leaders, staff and volunteers—from WCA Member Churches and others—attend one of our conferences or training events. Conferences offered on the Willow Creek campus in South Barrington, Illinois, include:

**Prevailing Church Conference:** Foundational training for staff and volunteers working to build a prevailing local church.

**Prevailing Church Workshops:** More than fifty strategic, day-long workshops covering seven topic areas that represent key characteristics of a prevailing church; offered twice each year.

**Promiseland Conference:** Children's ministries; infant through fifth grade.

**Student Ministries Conference:** Junior and senior high ministries.

**Willow Creek Arts Conference:** Vision and training for Christian artists using their gifts in the ministries of local churches.

**Leadership Summit:** Envisioning and equipping Christians with leadership gifts and respon-sibilities; broadcast live via satellite to eighteen cities across North America.

**Contagious Evangelism Conference:** Encouragement and training for churches and church leaders who want to be strategic in reaching lost people for Christ.

**Small Groups Conference:** Exploring how developing a church *of* small groups can play a vital role in developing authentic Christian community that leads to spiritual transformation.

To find out more about WCA conferences, visit our website at www.willowcreek.com.

## PREVAILING CHURCH REGIONAL WORKSHOPS

Each year the WCA team leads several, two-day training events in select cities across the United States. Some twenty day-long workshops are offered in topic areas including leadership, next-generation ministries, small groups, arts and worship, evangelism, spiritual gifts, financial stewardship, and spiritual formation. These events make quality training more accessible and affordable to larger groups of staff and volunteers.

To find out more about Prevailing Church Regional Workshops, visit our website at www.willowcreek.com.

### WILLOW CREEK RESOURCES™

Churches can look to Willow Creek Resources™ for a trusted channel of ministry tools in areas of leadership, evangelism, spiritual gifts, small groups, drama, contemporary music, financial stewardship, spiritual transformation, and more. For ordering information, call (800) 570-9812 or visit our website at www.willowcreek.com.

### WCA MEMBERSHIP

Membership in the Willow Creek Association as well as attendance at WCA Conferences is for churches, ministries, and leaders who hold to a historic, orthodox understanding of biblical Christianity. The annual church membership fee of $249 provides substantial discounts for your entire team on all conferences and Willow Creek Resources, networking opportunities with other outreach-oriented churches, a bimonthly newsletter, a subscription to the *Defining Moments* monthly audio journal for leaders, and more.

To find out more about WCA membership, visit our website at www.willowcreek.com.

### WILLOWNET (WWW.WILLOWCREEK.COM)

This Internet resource service provides access to hundreds of Willow Creek messages, drama scripts, songs, videos, and multimedia ideas. The system allows you to sort through these elements and download them for a fee.

Our website also provides detailed information on the Willow Creek Association, Willow Creek Community Church, WCA membership, conferences, training events, resources, and more.

### WILLOWCHARTS.COM (WWW.WILLOWCHARTS.COM)

Designed for local church worship leaders and musicians, WillowCharts.com provides online access to hundreds of music charts and chart components, including choir, orchestral, and horn sections, as well as rehearsal tracks and video streaming of Willow Creek Community Church performances.

### THE NET (HTTP://STUDENTMINISTRY.WILLOWCREEK.COM)

The NET is an online training and resource center designed by and for student ministry leaders. It provides an inside look at the structure, vision, and mission of prevailing student ministries from around the world. The NET gives leaders access to complete programming elements, including message outlines, dramas, small group questions, and more. An indispensable resource and networking tool for prevailing student ministry leaders!

### CONTACT THE WILLOW CREEK ASSOCIATION

If you have comments or questions, or would like to find out more about WCA events or resources, please contact us:

**Willow Creek Association**
P.O. Box 3188, Barrington, IL 60011-3188
Phone: (800) 570-9812 or (847) 765-0070
Fax: (888) 922-0035 or (847) 765-5046
Web: www.willowcreek.com

# TOUGH QUESTIONS

## Garry Poole and Judson Poling

"The profound insights and candor captured in these guides will sharpen your mind, soften your heart, and inspire you and the members of your group to find vital answers together."                    —Bill Hybels

This second edition of Tough Questions, designed for use in any small group setting, is ideal for use in seeker small groups. Based on more than five years of field-tested feedback, extensive revisions make this best-selling series easier to use and more appealing than ever for both participants and group leaders.

Softcover

| | |
|---|---|
| *How Does Anyone Know God Exists?* | ISBN 0-310-24502-8 |
| *What Difference Does Jesus Make?* | ISBN 0-310-24503-6 |
| *How Reliable Is the Bible?* | ISBN 0-310-24504-4 |
| *How Could God Allow Suffering and Evil?* | ISBN 0-310-24505-2 |
| *Don't All Religions Lead to God?* | ISBN 0-310-24506-0 |
| *Do Science and the Bible Conflict?* | ISBN 0-310-24507-9 |
| *Why Become a Christian?* | ISBN 0-310-24508-7 |
| *Leader's Guide* | ISBN 0-310-24509-5 |

*Pick up a copy at your favorite local bookstore today!*

**WILLOW CREEK** RESOURCES

**ZONDERVAN™**

GRAND RAPIDS, MICHIGAN 49530 USA

WWW.ZONDERVAN.COM

CPSIA information can be obtained
at www.ICGtesting.com
Printed in the USA
LVHW01s1914190318
570401LV00004B/35/P

9 780310 245025

# HOW DOES ANYONE KNOW GOD EXISTS?

Is Anybody Out There?

How Can Anyone Be S[...] God Exists?

What Is G[...] Like?

How C[...] People Believe [...] Miracles?

Does God Care What Happens to Us?

How Can a Person Get to Know God?

## GARRY POOLE

is the director of evangelism at Willow Creek Community Church in South Barrington, Illinois, an[...] author of *Seeker Sma[...] Groups, The Comple[...] Book of Questions,* and *The Three Habits of Highly Contagious Christians.*

# THE TOUGH QUESTIONS SERIES

*How can an all-powerful God allow suffering? Is Jesus really the only way to God? Why should I trust the Bible?*

Tough questions. Reasonable questions. The kinds of challenging questions you, or someone you know, may be asking, that are worth taking time to explore.

In six discussions designed to get small groups thinking and interacting, each guide in the Tough Questions series deals frankly with objections commonly raised about Christianity. You'll engage in the kind of spirited dialog that shows the Christian faith can stand up to scrutiny.

This revised edition of Tou[...] Questions, designed for u[...] in any small group setting, [...] ideal for seeker small grou[...] Based on more than five yea[...] of field-tested feedbac[...] extensive improvements ma[...] this bestselling series easier [...] use and more appealing th[...] ever for both participants a[...] group leaders.

ZONDERVAN.c[...]
AUTHORTRACK[...]
*follow your favorite au[...]*

RELIGION / Biblical Studies / Bible Study Gu[...]

**ZONDERVAN**

WILLOW CREEK RESOURCES
www.willowcreek.org

US $9.99
ISBN-10: 0-310-24502-8
ISBN-13: 978-0-310-24502-5

50999

9 780310 245025

# Health: A Common "Sensible" Approach

A guide to help weed through the daily nutritional and health contradictions

## Martin S Gildea
### DC, CFMP